—— Stuff Every ——
GRADUATE
—— Should Know ——

Library of Congress Cataloging in Publication Number: 2015946938

ISBN: 978-1-59474-860-8

Printed in China

Typeset in Goudy and Franklin Gothic

Designed by Andie Reid
Production management by John J. McGurk

Quirk Books
215 Church Street
Philadelphia, PA 19106
quirkbooks.com

10 9 8 7 6 5 4 3 2 1

—— Stuff Every ——
GRADUATE
—— Should Know ——

By Alyssa Favreau

QUIRK BOOKS
PHILADELPHIA

To my parents

Introduction: Welcome to the Real World

You did it. You got through it. You've run the gauntlet of exams, essays, and the occasional all-nighter and come out of it reasonably unscathed. You've got a diploma, a gown, and a nifty tasseled cap. (Fun fact to impress your friends: that hat is sometimes called a mortarboard or trencher.) Now it's time to gear up and succeed at this little thing called *the entire rest of your life*.

No pressure, right?

Gone are the days when grimy bedrooms, last-minute cram sessions, and uneaten pizza in the sink are acceptable parts of living. (Or, okay, mostly gone.) Adulthood means finding a job, making new friends, cooking, cleaning, and (I'm sorry) doing your taxes. You'll be learning a lot, but you don't need to feel overwhelmed—I promise.

Whether you need help finding your new dream home or polishing that resume to dazzle potential employers, you'll find what you need within these pages. (See that fun fact above? That's just the beginning.) Of course, this little book can't teach you *everything*, but, hey, no one ever took the world by storm without learning to wash their own socks first.

So congratulations, good luck, and go clean up that leftover Thai food. The real world awaits.

PERSONAL
STUFF

How to Build a Grown-Up Wardrobe

Whatever your personal style, the right clothes will make you feel cool, calm, and confident. Here's how to assemble, accessorize, and afford a grown-up wardrobe.

Shopping Like a Pro

- Even though flashy statement pieces are fun to wear (and to shop for), invest in basics—these should form two-thirds to three-quarters of your wardrobe. You'll spend less overall, and you won't have to sprint to the Laundromat weekly to get your one good shirt cleaned. Standards include button-down shirts, solid-color tops, dark jeans, a winter coat, a fall/ spring coat, a plain black dress, a suit, black socks, comfy underwear, workout wear, and lounging pants.

- Buy clothing that will last—and be prepared to spend more for it. Cheap fast-fashion chains are tempting, but the quality won't hold up and the looks go out of style in a flash. Similarly, resist the temptation to scoop up ill-fitting impulse buys, even if the price is low. "It hurts my ribcage but only costs $3" is not a valid rationalization.

- That said, some things—like fitted jackets, blazers, and blouses, or dress pants and skirts—will likely need to be tailored to fit properly. Budget an extra $10–$30 for alterations, especially if you'll wear them to work.

- Delicate materials like silk and cashmere are beautiful but also high maintenance (read: dry-clean only). If you don't have time to professionally launder clothes, don't buy them. Opt for machine-washable fabrics like cotton and synthetics. (Ditto for stuff that needs a lot of ironing: Be realistic! Do you even *own* an iron?)

- If you're shopping online, know your measurements (visit a tailor; don't just guess) and pay attention to user reviews and return policies. (Before ordering, google "[name of store] coupon" to find discounts.) The Internet's also great for fashionable plus-size clothing, pants with extra-long inseams, and hard-to-find styles.

- A good off-the-rack suit should have jacket sleeves that end exactly at your wrist and pant legs that fall with a single "break" (or fold) above the feet. Stick with wool or a wool-cashmere blend (no polyester!) in charcoal or navy for maximum versatility.

- Buy shoes made of real leather (or good-quality vegan leather), stitched (not glued) soles, and all organic (not synthetic) materials for laces. Pony up for a polishing kit to keep your leather looking good: polish once a month for occasional wear, once a week for shoes worn daily. A good pair can last a long time, so find a good cobbler to resole your kicks when necessary.

Dressing for Professional Success

- When you dress for a new job, err on the conservative side: a suit is usually fine, or *business casual* at least—that is, some variation on a button-down shirt, dark pants or skirt (with pantyhose), and clean shoes. Still unsure what to wear? Rule of thumb: dress like your boss.

- If you're wearing a suit jacket, here's a rundown of which button to fasten: sometimes (top button), always (middle), never (bottom).

- Heels, wacky patterns, bright shirts, and fun bow ties can be fine, but the goal is to appear competent rather than super stylish (though if you can pull off both, great!). Don't wear flip-flops, sneakers, or short shorts to work. Tank tops are okay under a blazer or neutral cardigan.

- Dressing business casual might mean covering up more than you're used to. Add a camisole under slightly sheer blouses, and invest in a neutral-colored office cardigan that can live at your desk in case of sudden arctic air-conditioning.

- Outfit yourself for the demands of the job. Wear footwear with good arch support if you're on your feet a lot, opt for layers if you work outside, bring a change of clothes if you work with children, and avoid flowing fabrics near machinery.

How to Take Care of Yourself When You're Sick

Since the last thing you want to do when you're bedridden is make complicated self-care decisions, here are some quick tips for combatting common ailments.

Colds

- Blow your nose instead of sniffing the phlegm back into your body.

- Gargle with warm salt water.

- Clear your sinuses by taking a hot shower; or fill a bowl with hot water, put your face over the steam, and cover both your head and the bowl with a towel.

- Drink lots of fluids.

- Wash your hands as often as possible.

- Eat foods that are easy on a sore throat, like soups and applesauce.

- Opt for nondrowsy daytime cold medicine if you need to stay alert, and sleep-friendly formulas when you want to catch some Z's.

- Clear your nasal passages using a neti pot and sinus rinse (available at most pharmacies; be sure to use distilled water or water that's been boiled and cooled to avoid parasites).

Flus

- As with a cold, hydrate, gargle, and unclog your sinuses.

- Prevention goes a long way: get a seasonal flu shot, wash your hands frequently, and stay away from that one coworker who showed up looking like a zombie.

- *Stay home.* Wait a full 24 hours after a fever abates before resuming your normal schedule.

- Try to eat a little something, even if you lack an appetite. A bit of soup or plain rice can help keep up your strength.

Fevers

- Get a thermometer (before you get sick, *ahem!*) and monitor your temperature to make sure it's returning to normal (98.6°F; 37°C).

- Rest and drink plenty of water. Popsicles will work.

- Both ibuprofen and acetaminophen can lower a fever, and most drug stores stock fever-specific options. Be sure to read all labels carefully.

- If you've got the chills, resist the urge to bundle up too much—you'll only increase your body temperature. Taking a lukewarm bath can help.

- Call a doctor if the fever doesn't respond to medication, is consistently above 103°F (39.4°C), or lasts for more than three days.

Menstrual Pain

- Stretching and yoga can help cramps. Also comforting are hot compresses or an electric heating pad applied to your lower abdomen. Make your own compress by filling a sock with uncooked rice and knotting the opening; microwave it for 1–2 minutes.

- Avoid alcohol and caffeine, which can dehydrate you and worsen symptoms.

- Take it easy. If you suffer from severe PMS, set a calendar alert to remind yourself to ease up and slow down.

- NSAIDs like ibuprofen or naproxen (not acetaminophen) will lessen uterine muscle contractions as well as leg, back, and head pain. You can use these medicines preventatively, too, but don't exceed the daily maximum dosage.

Food Poisoning

- Rest! Food poisoning usually passes through your system in a couple days. Stay well hydrated, too, to help your body get rid of the bacteria.

- Carbonated drinks can help settle a queasy stomach, but take small sips and avoid anything too cold, a shock to the system. Drinking sports drinks with electrolytes or sucking on ice chips also works.

- Stick to food that's easy on the stomach, like plain rice, soda crackers, bananas, cooked carrots, or oatmeal. Eat small quantities, and stop if the nausea returns. Avoid dairy products.

- If things get really serious, don't hesitate to call your doctor or go to the hospital. Some improperly cooked foods, like shellfish, can be extremely harmful.

General Tips

- The number one thing to remember—regardless of what's ailing you—is *get enough rest*. Put everything but the most pressing deadlines on hold, slow down, take care of yourself, and don't make things worse.

- Find someone you can rely on to take care of you when you need it: your parents or roommate if you live with them, a nearby friend or family member if you live solo.

- As soon as you move into a new place, stock up on these basics: painkillers (acetaminophen for headaches, ibuprofen for muscle pain), bandages, gastrointestinal medication, vitamin C, hand sanitizer, a thermometer, a topical ointment for cuts, and bandages.

- Read all dosage information and do not exceed the recommended amount. Sign up for automatic prescription refills if your pharmacy offers them, and program a daily phone alarm to remind you to take your meds.

- Take antibiotics only if a doctor has prescribed them. Finish the full course, even if you feel better sooner; doing so will ensure the infection is treated completely. Don't drink alcohol while on antibiotics—you risk serious liver damage.

- Going to a real live doctor before your symptoms worsen is always a good idea. Trying to diagnose yourself with tools like WebMD is dicey and might just convince you that you're dying of some horrible disease (when in fact you just have the flu). Drop-in clinics (sometimes attached to a pharmacy) can address minor illnesses like strep throat, pink eye, and sinus infections.

- If you are experiencing severe pain or a high fever, can't keep down fluids, or have injured yourself, go to an emergency room.

How to Stay in Shape

You know exercise is good for you, but whether you're starting a stressful new job or spending a lot of time with Netflix, maintaining a postgrad fitness regimen can be tough. Here's how to defeat laziness and keep yourself going strong.

- Know yourself: If you prefer to work out alone, try swimming laps, cycling, or a one-on-one boxing lesson. If you'd rather be part of a group, a water-aerobics class or swim team, runners' group, or basketball league might be better. If you have bad knees, asthma, or depth perception problems, or if you need a wheelchair-friendly activity, research the types of exercise that will work for you to narrow down your options and keep you safe.

- The fancy gym with the army of personal trainers might be tempting, but community rec centers and YMCA chapters will almost always be cheaper. Universities may offer classes to local nonstudents, and yoga studios often have by-donation community classes for charity. If budgets can't budge, pick up an inexpensive gym mat and take to YouTube for exercise videos.

- Pressed for time? Try a circuit workout: 30 seconds each of jumping jacks, wall sits, push-ups, chair step-ups, squats, triceps chair dips, ab planks, running in place, and lunges, with 10-second breaks in between. Phew!

- Fit exercise into your schedule wherever it makes sense, even if it's a quick 30-minute session during a lunch break or a late-night yoga class to relax before bed. If the workout is convenient, you're more likely to do it.

- Workouts that fulfill two objectives may be easier to stick with. Joining an amateur softball league will win you new friends. Dance classes can double as quality couple time. Treadmill workouts are opportunities to catch up on Netflix or podcasts.

- Don't feel intimidated. Exercise is literally for every body, whether you're a former teenage athlete or you've never run a mile in your life. Lots of people start new sports as adults, so head to that roller derby info session. If you're nervous, talk to the instructor beforehand—they'll love an eager newcomer.

- Don't get down on yourself. If you lapse a little, the least helpful thing is to beat yourself up. Just move on and start fresh.

Medical Care 101

In an ideal world, every cut and cough would be treated promptly by an affordable medical provider. But in the real world, taking good care of yourself isn't easy to figure out—especially if you're already feeling woozy. (For more on insurance, see page 110.) Here's how to stay healthy, happy, and sane.

What kind of doctor do I need?

- *General practitioners* (GPs) perform check-ups and treat illnesses in the beginning stages, referring patients to specialists if a problem progresses.

- *Gynecologists* deal broadly with the female reproductive organs, while *obstetricians* primarily handle childbirth and neonatal care. Many doctors work in both fields simultaneously (known as OB/GYNs).

- *Specialists* (podiatrists, dermatologists, allergists, etc.) concentrate on a specific body part or system. Your GP will refer you to one if needed.

- *Psychiatrists* diagnose and treat mental disorders and may specialize in one area, such as psychotherapy, eating disorders, or dementia-related problems. Unlike *therapists*, psychiatrists can prescribe medication.

- *Emergency room doctors and nurses* are responsible for triaging patients, assessing the problem, and beginning care. Once admitted to a hospital, a patient is usually sent to other doctors in appropriate departments, depending on the problem.

- *Walk-in clinicians*, whether doctors or nurse practitioners, work in facilities that accept patients without an appointment. Such clinics may focus on emergency care, immunization, or sexual health and often offer basic medical services only.

How do I even find a doctor?

- Ask around for recommendations—friends and coworkers are more trustworthy than anonymous online reviews.

- Use an online search engine like ZocDoc, WebMD, or DocASAP to find doctors near your house or office.

- Browse your insurance company's Internet portal for doctors guaranteed to be in-network.

- Find a doctor *before* you get sick. The last thing you want to do when you're ill is spend time researching practitioners.

When do I have to see my doctor?

- **Once a year for a checkup.** Preventative care is the easiest way to maintain good health. For some, that includes an annual gynecological exam and Pap smear. Some general practitioners will perform these; others will direct you to an OB/GYN.

- **At least once a year for teeth cleaning.** Nobody likes going to the dentist, but nobody likes root canals or gum surgery, either. Regular cleanings are the best prevention.

- **Every few months/partners if you're sexually active.** Clinics can handle Pap smears and urine tests (sometimes for free or at reduced cost for young people). If you're experiencing any symptoms, don't wait to get them checked.

- **If you're managing a chronic condition.** Visit your doctor more frequently if you have an ongoing condition like diabetes, heart problems, or chronic pain. Even if your treatment regimen is working, checking in is wise.

- **If you're dealing with mental health issues.** A psychiatrist will diagnose and treat problems like severe depression, anxiety, or mood disorders and can prescribe medication if appropriate.

- **After an accident.** Even if you feel fine! Everything from concussions to a broken toe can cause serious complications if not patched up properly.

- **For a severe allergic reaction.** If you experience hives, nausea/vomiting, shortness of breath, or swelling after contact with an allergen (food, medication, bug bite or sting, etc.), get to an emergency room STAT!

- **If you're pregnant.** An obstetrician will make sure you're getting adequate nutrition and rest and monitor your baby's health, too.

How to Handle Depression

Though it often seems like everyone else is doing fine, depression is common. According to a 2011 survey by the National Institute of Mental Health, 30 percent of college students reported feeling "so depressed it was difficult to function" sometime in the previous year. After graduation, it can be especially hard to leave student life behind and figure out where to go next in your "adult" life. *You are not alone.* Many of us experience this feeling of loss or sadness. Here's how to make your mental health a priority during such a tumultuous transition.

Deal with Your Damn Feelings

1. **Be aware of your damn feelings.** Common symptoms of depression include (but are not

limited to) a sense of hopelessness or helplessness; changes in sleep patterns, appetite, and weight; loss of energy; decreased interest in daily activities; problems with concentration; feelings of self-hatred; and suicidal thoughts. You might not experience all these symptoms, but recognize that this state of mind isn't something you can just shake off.

2. **Share your damn feelings.** You might want nothing more than to stay under the covers for a cartoon-watching marathon, but force yourself to hang out with friends (or, you know, invite them over to watch cartoons). Tell family members what you're going through and ask them for advice. Don't feel embarrassed about needing help. Depression is isolating, but having a caring support system goes a long way toward making you realize you are not alone.

3. **Talk to a therapist about your damn feelings.** Therapy can be extremely helpful, and seeking help is *not* an admission of defeat, weakness, or insanity. Research local services

(*Psychology Today* offers an online search engine of providers, as do many insurance companies) to find someone who works with young adults or your specific situation. You might not find a good fit right away, so try a few therapists until you both "click."

And Don't Forget to...

- **Take care of yourself.** Doing nice things for yourself is a matter of self-preservation, not self-indulgence. Make happiness your top priority. Listen to your favorite music. Bake brownies. Play Tetris, knit a sweater. Whatever raises your spirits.

- **Avoid self-medicating.** Don't use alcohol or drugs to deal with how you're feeling. You might think these will bring immediate stress relief, but in the long run substance abuse is likely to deepen and may in fact *cause* depression.

- **Be patient.** Remember that life doesn't fall into place right away. Jobs take a while to materialize. Friends move away. Parents can be overbearing. Maybe you feel like you've taken a massive step backward, but don't despair. Life doesn't always move consistently forward or at a constant pace. You're doing fine.

LIVING
STUFF

Apartment Hunting 101

Congratulations—you're moving out! Either you've been cozy with your parents or cramped in a dorm room, but now it's time to find four walls and a roof to call your own. Terrifying? Just a little. These tips will help you move on.

Finding a Place

Researching apartments can feel like job hunting crossed with hitting the dating scene—i.e., painful—but it doesn't have to be. Here's how to search smarter.

- **Know what you can afford.** The rule of thumb is not to spend more than 30 percent of your income on rent, but it's okay to go over if you can swing it. Create a budget (see page 115) to see what your income allows. Don't cut it too close, though—you can't just *not pay* rent.

- **Consider a roomie.** It's usually cheaper to pay for half of a two-bedroom, and you and your roommate can also split chores and costs like utilities and groceries. Either take an empty room in an existing group-living situation or find a roommate and together search for an apartment. Make sure you are both on the same page about routines, quiet times, bill paying, dish doing, and overnight guests. Don't hesitate to ask candidates for proof of employment—don't get stuck paying rent for two!

Warning

Before you bunk with a friend, make sure they meet your "good roommate" criteria. Living with your bestie can seem like a great idea—it's certainly less time consuming than vetting someone new—but if you're going to snipe over dirty dishes, loud music, or lagging bills, you might be left with nothing but a broken friendship.

- **Hit up Craig and his glorious list.** Seriously, online listings (Craigslist, Zillow, Padmapper, or a local alternative) are your new best friends. Plug your maximum rent into the search engine, then check early and often. If you still live in the town where you attended college, check the school classifieds.

- **Ask around.** Friends or colleagues might know rentals that haven't yet been advertised. (Bonus: if the person looking for a roommate is a friend of a friend, you already have a reference.) Make use of special-interest Facebook groups—religiously observant or queer friendly, for example—to find living situations to suit your lifestyle.

- **Do a drive-by.** Sometimes landlords don't bother advertising on Craigslist, so if a neighborhood strikes your fancy, bike or walk around the area and search for rent signs.

- **Don't get ripped off.** Everyone you deal with should be open, friendly but not pushy, and willing to provide whatever information you need. Beware when your calls or e-mails go unanswered, especially if you're asking important questions. If a listing was posted by a company, research it: simply google "[company name] scam." Share as little personal information as you can and bring a friend when visiting the apartment (or at least tell people where you're going). Don't wire anyone money, and walk away if there are any red flags. You have other options.

- **Call, don't text.** Things move fast, so as soon as you see a good space, *call* the landlord immediately and ask to see it.

Sizing Up Your Prospective Future Home

Arrange to see the apartment you will be renting—not a model unit in the building or another property entirely. (Pro tip: Never sign for an apartment sight unseen!) Consider these factors.

- What's the 'hood like? An area with a bunch of settled families will be nice and quiet, but probably have fewer cool bars (and higher rent). A more up-and-coming part of town will be cheaper, but maybe not as safe.

- How close is it to work? Is there parking?

- How close are key amenities—grocery store, bus stop, Laundromat, doctor's office, park, decent pizza delivery? Be realistic about how far you're willing to travel.

- Is there room for your furniture? Will your stuff fit through the door/up the stairs? (Remember that "Pivot!" scene in *Friends*? Don't do that.)

- Are pets allowed?

- How much natural light comes into the space?

- Are the kitchen facilities adequate for your cooking habits?

- Do your roommates like the place, too? Remember, it'll be a loooong lease to ride out if anyone (including you) feels pushed into the living situation.

- Is everything in good, clean, working condition? Thoroughly check:

    ○ Light fixtures

    ○ Electrical sockets

    ○ Taps and plumbing (it's not weird to give the toilet a test flush)

    ○ Phone jack

    ○ Heating and air-conditioning

    ○ Included appliances

    ○ Storage space

- Locks

- Grout in kitchen and bathroom

- Cupboards/cupboards doors

- Smoke detectors

- Deadbolt locks, if the apartment opens onto a street

- Window bars, if you're on the first floor

- No mold, water damage, or weird smells

- No sign of insects or pests

- How long has the landlord had the property? Who does repairs? Get a name and phone number, and ask about past problems.

- When is rent due? How do you pay—cash or check, in person, by mail, or online?

- How soon can you get phone, Internet, and cable service?

- Who handles trash and recycling?

- Do you have access to common spaces—backyards, balconies, gym, storage rooms, bike racks? How are those monitored or shared?

- Can you receive packages? (Some buildings direct large deliveries to the nearest post office for pickup, which can be a real pain if you work during the day.)

- Why is the current/previous tenant moving? Ask for references from past or current renters of the unit or in the building. It's a red flag if a landlord isn't willing to share names.

Reading and Signing the Lease

Basically, a lease says "this person will pay this much for this apartment." But really it's a little more complicated. Here's how to read the fine print.

- **Read the entire document.** Attentively. The lease should state the amount of rent you'll be paying, the date by which the rent must be paid (typically the first of every month), the appliances included in the rental, who is responsible for repairs, what happens if you violate the lease, and whether you're allowed to have pets, paint the walls, or hang things off your porch. Ask questions and raise concerns before you sign. All additions and amendments to the lease should be initialed by both parties.

- **Bring credentials.** Expect to have your credit history checked (usually for a charge, which shouldn't exceed $30 or so). Your landlord may also ask for proof of employment (pay stubs or employer contact info) and/or a letter of reference (especially for a fancier place). And it never hurts to bring photo ID.

- **To sign or co-sign?** Having your lease co-signed means that someone else will be legally responsible for the rent if you fall behind (which is handy if you don't have a steady paycheck or good credit history). Most first-time renters use their parents, who are usually comfortable with bearing such a legal responsibility for their offspring.

- **Pay up.** You'll typically have to pay the first and last month's rent and/or a security deposit (usually the amount of an additional month's rent) up-front. Before you're required to pay, ask whether the landlord accepts checks—you don't want to get stuck waiting a couple days to withdraw the necessary cash.

- **Know your commitment.** A one-year lease is typical. If you don't plan to stick around for the full term, ask ahead of time if the landlord will let you sublet (i.e., allow someone else to live in the space and pay rent, either to you or to the landlord). Also find out how much your landlord can legally raise the rent every year—in many places, around 5 percent is the norm.

How to Move

Moving is a total pain in the butt, but try to view it less as a really annoying chore and more as the perfect opportunity to streamline all your possessions. The following steps will make the process as painless as possible and help you lighten your load—literally.

- Make three piles—Keep, Donate, Trash—and start sorting. Now is not the time for sentimentality, so be realistic about how often you'll need that copy of Shakespeare's sonnets or those purple Mardi Gras beads.

- Don't put your bed (or other essentials) up for sale until a couple days before you move unless you have another place to sleep (or don't mind the floor).

- Got too much food? Throw a Let's Eat Everything in My Cupboards dinner party. Closet overflowing? Host a clothing swap party. Donate anything leftover to a local charity.

- Once you've pared down, it's time to pack. Most businesses (especially liquor stores) will hand over cardboard boxes if you ask nicely; in a pinch, hardware and big-box stores sell them for a moderate price. Pack clothes in luggage, rolling (not folding) garments to save space. Load soft items like linens in large garbage bags (double-bag in case of rips).

- Box things according to where they'll go in your new place, labeling the sides clearly so you and your friends/movers know where to put them.

- Carefully wrap breakable items like plates and cups, further protecting them with towels and bed sheets. Put soaps, shampoos, nail polishes, and other spillables in plastic bags.

- Distribute weight. Don't put an entire bookshelf's worth of books in one box—you won't be able to lift it. Fill it halfway, then pad out the rest with lighter items.

- You have a few vehicular options. Friends and their cars are wonderful if you ask nicely and supply pizza at the end of the day. A you-drive-it rental truck works if you can maneuver the vehicle and carry boxes yourself. Movers will take care of *everything* (sometimes even packing, though you'll want to supervise) but cost much more—investigate student mover companies for an affordable option. Don't rely on public transit or taxis unless you want to make a driver grumpy.

- Some stuff just won't survive the trip. Budget extra cash to replace things like cleaning supplies.

How to Coexist with Roommates

Whether you're best friends intent on spending all your free time together or civil strangers who happen to share a home, a positive stress-free roommate relationship is the best kind. Here's how to stay happy, friendly, and sane when problems arise.

Problem: Your roommate is all up in your business and you can't stand it.

Solution: The key to living well communally is setting clear boundaries beforehand (quiet hours, off-limits spaces like bedrooms, shared food, etc.), but if your roomies accidentally use all your expensive salon shampoo while making noise after midnight and hogging the bathroom, don't flip! Give them the benefit of the doubt— they probably just didn't know. Politely point out the transgression, remind them you're not mad (even if you are, a little), and establish a clear protocol for similar situations going forward.

Problem: You're doing all the chores.

Solution: What we have here is a failure to communicate. One person's "clean" is another person's "barely touched with a sponge." Approach your roommate with a friendly smile and discuss what should be cleaned and when. If things still go unscrubbed, talk again and institute a structured official system (yes, you can tack a chore chart on the fridge if you want). If it gets *really* nasty, consider asking your 'mates to pitch in for maid service.

Problem: Resentment is brewing and everyone is tense.

Solution: Talk early, clearly, and often. Consider having regular house meetings (especially if you're three or more people) when complaints and questions can be aired—an established forum to deal with issues will make it easier to address perpetual milk stealing or the couple whose nighttime fun is messing up everyone else's sleep schedules. If things get heated or worse, remind everyone that you're speaking up because you want a happy household. Be willing to compromise, for the love of the group's mental health. Sometimes you get to stand firm on everyone flushing the toilet, other times you'll have to cave and buy the detergent because you use it more than anyone else. That's (roommate) life.

Problem: You've really tried to give this thing a shot, but your living situation is just not working.

Solution: Some people don't get along in close quarters. Maybe you make good friends but terrible roommates, maybe you didn't anticipate awful significant others or just how bothersome loud midnight snack-making could be. If it's not a good situation, moving out could save the friendship and your sanity. Just pack it in responsibly: give at least one or two months' heads-up, and if you still have time on the lease, find a subletter that your roommate is comfortable with. Don't steal away in the night and leave your roomie scrambling to cover costs you signed up for.

How to Deal with Living with Your Parents

It happens: many recent graduates move back in with their parents. Yes, it allows you to save on rent while figuring out your next step, but that doesn't make it an easy option. Learn how to avoid these common pitfalls.

Problem: Your parents think the rules from your teenage years still apply.

Solution: Sit down early and outline the expectations of both parties, and then meet in the middle. If you don't want a curfew, agree to tell your parents where you're going at night. Don't be unreasonable—your parents are just not going to let you throw giant house parties—but do stick up for yourself and then earn their trust by being responsible and keeping to your end of the bargain.

Problem: *You* think the rules from when you were a teenager still apply.

Solution: Just because you're home doesn't mean you have to act like a child. Do your laundry (sorry!). Pitch in with cooking, shopping, and cleaning. Respect your parents and don't sass them (at least not at your former I'm-sixteen-and-misunderstood levels). If you've agreed to pay rent, pay it. You are now roommates, and any consideration you'd give to someone you're not related to should be extended to your parents.

Problem: No one is accustomed to sharing space anymore, and you're all stepping on one another's toes.

Solution: Take up residence in a basement, attic, or garage, if possible, to get more independence and give everyone some breathing room. If you can't find physical space, work around one another: maybe you need a bathroom schedule so you aren't all scrambling to shower before work, maybe a room needs to be designated as a work-only quiet space, maybe your brother needs to stop hoarding the peanut butter. Every family has a different dynamic, but some things apply universally (bedroom doors must be knocked on before entering!). Still stressed about space? Call a family meeting and address matters in a neutral setting.

Problem: You get too comfortable and lose sight of your ambitions.

Solution: Home has all sorts of distractions (that N64 is not going to play itself), but don't give in. Find ways to give structure to your day. If you're job-hunting, force yourself to start at a certain time and go until you've gotten in a few productive hours. Still figuring out your next step? Get a part-time job or volunteer. Leaving the house will keep you from feeling stuck and help stave off postgraduation depressive feelings (for more on those, see page 32).

Problem: Your parents are super judgmental.

Solution: Your parents will be judgmental—it's kind of part of the job description. They may take issue with aspects of your lifestyle ("Honey, are you sure you need to stay up past 2 a.m.?"), think you're going about your job hunt the wrong way ("When I was your age I marched into the building with my résumé and stayed there until they hired me!"), or just worry about you (nonstop). Overbearing remarks are easier to deal with if you can see the light at the end of the tunnel, so stay sane with an exit strategy— and then focus on it. Also, don't write off their complaints as mere nagging. If you're whining about an empty fridge but haven't offered to grocery shop, then your parents might be kind of…right.

How to Complain to Your Landlord

The tenant/landlord relationship can be tricky. After all, you are relying on each other for basic needs like housing and income, and sometimes things go wrong.

Speaking up isn't necessarily *complaining*. The landlord's job is to fix problems, and you're passing along needed information. Be polite, respectful, and grateful when things are taken care of quickly. Here are some ways to keep communication flowing.

- **Be in touch.** An informal text message is an appropriate way to raise a complaint if your landlord is an individual rather than a company and you communicate mostly via texts. If you're dealing with a holdings company, think you may eventually have to take legal action, or simply feel the need for added gravitas, a formal letter is a better method. When drafting the letter, make sure it's polite and to the point. Include your name, address and unit number, the date, the problem, the solution you're expecting, and whatever portion of the lease agreement makes it the other party's responsibility. If you're *really* concerned, send it via registered mail.

- **Be timely.** The sooner your landlord knows about an issue, the faster it'll get fixed. Even if the repair is technically your responsibility, keep your landlord in the loop. It might be better to get a recommendation for a trusted tradesperson rather than tinker away at a door that won't close tight.

- **Be available.** Many landlords have spare keys and will work without you at home, but it's always a good idea to be on the premises when repairs happen, especially if outside contractors, like exterminators or plumbers, will be entering your home.

- **Brush up on legalese.** Google "tenant rights [your area]" and familiarize yourself with what you can and cannot expect from a landlord (many states have a downloadable tenant's handbook). Don't threaten to withhold rent until your unacceptable living situation improves, for example, unless you're sure you have the legal right to do so.

- **Implement a three-strike rule.** For conflicts between you and your neighbor with the penchant for wild Wednesday night parties, don't bring the landlord into the mix right away. Ask them to quiet down in person and *then* go to the landlord if nothing changes. "I've asked 4B three times not to leave cigarette butts everywhere, but they're not listening" is much easier to work with than a tenant who merely tattles.

How to Make a Meal Plan and Grocery Shop

Think of a meal plan as a road map for food. Planning all the meals you'll eat for a week can save you a long and pizza-heavy transition period after your dining hall life (though, real talk, pizza is delicious). It'll also help you stop wasting food and avoid shopping five times a week.

- Draw a diagram (or use a day planner or even your smartphone calendar) with space for all the meals you'll eat.

- Next, look at your calendar and determine when you'll have time to shop and cook. If you're home only a few nights a week, plan to cook large meals that keep for several days (like stews and curries) and portion them out.

- Make healthy choices. Focus on fruits and vegetables (the darker the color, the more nutrient-rich the food) and whole grains, plus lean meats, fish, beans, eggs, and nuts for protein, dairy products for calcium, and as few saturated and trans fats as possible.

- Seek balance. Don't swear off junk food forever, but do try to offset Friday's pizza and beer with meals full of leafy greens on other days.

- Be realistic and flexible. You might not get home early enough to whip up that roast chicken, so stock up on quick meal options.

- Love your leftovers! Make double batches of recipes and freeze them for later (one-quart yogurt containers work great for storage). Pack a lunch-sized portion of dinner while you're washing up and the next day's midday meal is taken care of.

Based on your plan (see pages 64–65 for an example), make a shopping list, including any staples you're running low on. Having this list will make grocery shopping faster, less frequent, and clear of impulse purchases. Here are more tips for shopping smart.

- Seasonal produce is more affordable and hasn't been shipped halfway across the world. Shopping farmers' markets can also keep down costs, especially if you want to eat organic.

- Stock up on staples that don't spoil quickly. At the market, scoop as much rice, coffee, flour, and other dry goods as you need; at a big-box discounter, grab massive quantities of things like paper towels and toothpaste. Just make sure you can store (and carry!) everything you buy.

- Smaller markets, bodegas, or convenience stores are just that—convenient, and often more expensive. Then again, some mom-and-pop grocery stores are treasure troves of good deals on nonperishables, so check prices!

- Forget clipping coupons. Many chain groceries now have smartphone apps that let you collect points and cash in on deals.

- "Shortcut" foods like cooked chicken strips and grated cheese are convenient but often more expensive. Weigh time vs. money carefully!

Sample Meal Plan

	MONDAY	TUESDAY	WEDNESD
BREAKFAST	Cereal and orange slices	Eggs, toast, baked tomato	Cereal a orange sl
AM SNACK			
LUNCH	Turkey and avocado sandwich	Walnut, spinach, and blueberry salad	Leftover
PM SNACK	Smoked almonds		Carrot sti and hum
DINNER	Sunday leftovers	Chili and green salad	Kale, car and caulif stir-fry
DESSERT			

URSDAY	FRIDAY	SATURDAY	SUNDAY
ffin on e go	Oatmeal and an apple	Fruit and yogurt, bagel	
ola bar grapes			French toast and berries
, snow eas	Sushi with coworkers	Cucumber quinoa salad	
shroom asta	Fish burger and fries and beer	Mustard chicken and rice	Big batch of veggie stew
fee and ownie		Frozen yogurt	

Eight Cooking Techniques to Master

You've decided what you'll be eating and stocked the necessary ingredients. Time to get cooking!

1. **Making a basic vinaigrette**
   In the bottom of a large bowl (big enough to fit all the salad ingredients), add 1 tablespoon of red wine vinegar, 4 tablespoons of olive oil, and a pinch each of salt and pepper. Whisk together (you can use a fork!). Optional additions: herbs (like rosemary), a dollop of grainy mustard, or a squeeze of lemon juice.

2. **Boiling the perfect hard-cooked egg**
   Place eggs in a large saucepan and add enough cool water to cover by 1 inch. Over medium heat, bring the water to a steady boil, then remove the pan from the heat, cover, and let it sit for 12 minutes. Prepare an ice bath (ice cubes and water in a small bowl). Drain eggs

in a colander and dunk them in the ice bath
to stop cooking and cool them. Then dry,
peel, and enjoy.

3. Tear-free onion cutting

With a sharp knife, cut the onion in half,
then peel off the skin and lay each half flat
side down on a cutting board. Cut off the
stem (but not the roots—they'll hold the
layers in place), and make cuts perpendicular
to the root about ¼ inch apart. Turn each
half 90 degrees and cut again, perpendicular
to your first cuts, resulting in perfect(ish)
little cubes.

4. Seasoning *everything*

Herbs and spices are an important part of
what makes food taste good. Everyone's palate
is different, so don't be afraid to experiment—
though the myriad choices can overwhelm
the inexperienced cook. Just remember:
practice makes perfect. To get started, use the
handy chart on page 68 to figure out what flavor combinations work best. Note that dried
herbs have a more concentrated flavor than
fresh herbs, so if you substitute fresh for dried

	MEAT	POULTRY	FISH	VEGETABLES	SOUPS
BASIL	X	X	X	X	X
CINNAMON		X			X
CLOVES	X				X
FENNEL	X		X	X	
GARLIC	X	X	X	X	X
GINGER	X	X	X	X	X
MUSTARD	X	X	X	X	X
OREGANO		X	X	X	X
PARSLEY	X	X	X	X	X
ROSEMARY	X	X	X	X	X
SAGE	X	X	X	X	X
SESAME		X	X	X	

in a recipe, you will need about three times as much to achieve the same flavor.

5. Thawing frozen meat

The safest way is to defrost it in the fridge overnight. If you're in a hurry, remove the meat from its package, put it on a plate, and run it under cool water in the sink. Micro-wave defrosting should be a last resort—you might accidentally start cooking it! Always cook meat to the proper temperature: 165°F (74°C) for poultry, 160°F (71°C) for ground meats, 145°F (63°C) for steaks, pork, and fish.

6. Cooking rice

In a medium saucepan, bring 1½ cups of water to a boil. Stir in 1 cup of long-grain white rice (basmati, for example) and ½ teaspoon of salt. Reduce heat to medium-high and bring to a boil, then reduce to low, cover the pan, and cook for 16–18 minutes, until the rice is tender and has absorbed the water (you'll see little holes made by the steam when it's ready). Remove from heat and leave covered for 10 minutes, then fluff rice with a fork.

7. Steaming vegetables

Clean and peel the vegetables and cut them into uniform bite-sized chunks. Add 1 inch of water to a saucepan equipped with a steamer basket. Put veggie pieces in the steamer basket, ensuring they're not touching the water. Bring water to a boil over high heat, then reduce heat to medium and cover. After a few minutes, poke the thickest part of the vegetables with a fork to see if they're tender. Remove from the heat while they're still a bit crunchy—they'll keep cooking and be perfect by the time they're eaten. If you're cooking different veggies together, remember that denser ones, like carrots or potatoes, cook more slowly than the likes of mushrooms or peppers, so add the quicker-cooking vegetables later.

AVERAGE COOKING TIMES	
Spinach	3 minutes
Broccoli, green beans	5–7 minutes
Carrots, potatoes, squash	10–20 minutes

Necessary Equipment for Every Kitchen

Sharp knives (8- or 9-inch chef's knife, paring knife, and serrated knife)

Spatula

Ladle

Tongs

Wooden spoon

Cutting board

Pots (one big and one small, with lids)

Nonstick frying pan or wok

Mixing bowls

Measuring cups and spoons

Rimmed baking sheet

Grater

Strainer or colander

Pyrex or ceramic baking dishes

Muffin tins, cake pans, pie tins, and other specialty bakeware

Handheld electric mixer

8. Super fast, super easy pizza dough

Want pizza? This recipe doesn't require yeast or hours for the dough to rise.

2 cups self-rising flour (or 2 cups all-purpose flour plus 3 teaspoons baking powder), plus a little extra for kneading

1 teaspoon salt

2 teaspoons baking powder

²/₃ cup water

1 tablespoon olive oil

Your favorite toppings

Preheat oven to 425°F (218°C) and line a baking sheet with parchment paper. Combine flour, salt, and baking powder in a bowl. In a glass measuring cup, mix together water and oil. Slowly pour liquid ingredients into dry ingredients, mixing with your hands as you go.

Sprinkle extra flour on the counter, transfer dough to the floured surface, and knead dough (working it with your knuckles) for about 5 minutes, until it's spreadable but not sticky. Place dough in the center of the lined baking sheet. With a rolling pin, smooth bottle, or the palm of your hand, spread the dough to 1 inch thick.

Add toppings and bake for about 15–20 minutes, checking frequently to make sure it doesn't burn.

Outside-the-Box Topping Ideas

Sliced onions, tomatoes, and/or green peppers

Sliced fresh fruit like apples and pears

Chopped fresh herbs like basil or thyme

Chopped garlic

Delicate greens like spinach or arugula

Chopped roast chicken

Sautéed sausage or bacon

Chopped and blanched/roasted root vegetables like potatoes, sweet potatoes, or winter squash

Chopped and blanched leafy greens such as kale or swiss chard

Basil or sun-dried tomato pesto

Sliced fresh mozzarella, crumbled goat cheese, or dollops of ricotta

Thinly sliced fennel

Chopped marinated artichoke hearts

Chopped pitted olives, such as kalamata

Culinary Lingo Cheat Sheet

Here in the real world, your culinary repertoire is no longer confined to whatever can be microwaved or reconstituted with boiling water. Familiarize yourself with these terms.

Bake: Cook food—often pastries or breads—in an oven using dry heat.

Blanch: Boil food and then quickly submerge it in cold water to immediately stop cooking and keep things crisp.

Boil: Cook food by submerging in hot bubbling water.

Broil: Cook food using heat from above. This method is useful when you want to brown something quickly, like cheese on top of a lasagna. You'll find the broiler at the top of the oven or in a drawer underneath the oven.

Brown: Cook food in an oiled pan until a golden brown crust forms.

Chop: Cut ingredients into rough, fairly large chunks.

Dice: Cut ingredients such as onions (see page 67) and

other vegetables into small, square pieces.

Fry: Cook food in oil, either in a pan (pan-frying) or by fully submerging it in hot oil (deep-frying).

Grill: Cook food with a heat source that comes from underneath, like a barbecue.

Sauté: Cook food on the stovetop with high heat, moving it around so it doesn't burn (essentially making things jump—but not too high—in the pan).

Simmer: Cook food in a liquid (sauce or broth) on the stovetop, using low heat so that small bubbles rise to the surface.

Steam: Suspend food over evaporating water, letting the hot air cook it.

How to Clean House

You can't live in teenage squalor forever. A once-a-week cleaning will keep your house or apartment from being, well, squalid. Hopefully you've cleaned at some point in your life, but here are basic pointers for tidying up.

Items You Will Need

- Broom with flexible bristles and dust pan

- Vacuum cleaner, either a full-sized model or a handheld one to pair with the broom

- All-purpose surface cleaner

- Window washing liquid

- Cleaning rags

- Duster

- Plunger (don't wait to buy one until you need one!)

- Toilet bowl scrub brush

- Dish soap

- Sponge and scrubbing pad (one set for dishes, one for appliances and spills)

Baking Soda, the Miracle Worker

Baking soda is a simple, natural all-purpose cleaner that can do many things: unclog drains, clean dishwashers and coffee makers (just run it through the machine to make it sparkle), freshen up fridges and carpets (sprinkle it over a rug, let sit for a few minutes, and then vacuum up), and even be used with water to mop floors.

Items You May Need

- Snow shovel

- Mop, bucket, and liquid floor cleaner, or spritzing mop with disposable pads

- Stepladder

- Reusable spray bottle

- Wood polish spray and oil soap for furniture

- Adhesive remover (like Goo Gone)

- Rubber gloves

Basic Cleaning Techniques

- Tidy up paperwork, clothes, electronics, etc., before cleaning surfaces with a sponge so you don't have to work around piles of stuff.

- Clean from top to bottom. Start with cabinets, high shelves, and cobwebby ceiling corners, and then sweep dust and crumbs off the floors.

- Sweep everything—don't forget spaces under furniture—into one big pile and either collect it in a dustpan or vacuum it up. (Most of the buildup will be in the kitchen and high-traffic areas like a front hallway.)

- Mop tiled floors with a mixture of hot water and floor cleaner, wringing the mop as you go. Then clean the mop and finish by going over the floor again with plain water.

- Sinks, showers, and bathtubs naturally accumulate soap scum, so be proactive and clean them regularly with a sponge and a good surface cleaner. If your faucets or showerheads are blocked, tie a baggie full of white vinegar around them to dissolve the grime overnight.

- Dirty toilets are *the grossest*. Use a toilet brush to clean the inside of the bowl. Clean the outside with a sponge and spray (don't forget the underside of the seat!). Apply liquid toilet bowl cleaner around the bowl at the top, and flush to distribute it.

- Wipe spatters off the stovetop and kitchen counters as soon as you're done cooking to prevent caked-on gunk.

- To save money (and paper), use sponges, cloths, and rags (aka cut-up old T-shirts) instead of paper towels—but throw them out when they get shredded or smell bad.

- Besides your weekly (okay, *biweekly*) cleanup, don't forget less frequent but still important chores like sweeping behind large furniture and appliances, washing your mattress cover (seriously, get a mattress cover), flipping your mattress, tidying outdoor areas, and cleaning inside cupboards and drawers.

- Warning: Never mix cleaning products containing ammonia with ones that contain bleach—you'll create *very toxic* fumes!

GUIDE TO LAUNDRY TAG SYMBOLS

WASHING

1. 2. 3. 4. 5.

1. machine wash cold 2. machine wash warm
3. machine wash hot 4. hand wash 5. do not wash

DRYING

1. 2. 3. 4. 5. 6. 7. 8.

1. tumble dry no heat 2. tumble dry low heat 3. tumble dry
medium heat, 4. tumble dry high heat, 5. do not tumble dry
6. line dry 7. drip dry 8. dry flat

IRONING

1. 2. 3. 4. 5.

1. iron steam or dry with low heat 2. iron steam or dry with
medium heat 3. iron steam or dry with high heat
4. do not iron with steam 5. do not iron

BLEACHING

1. △ 2.  3. ✖

1. bleach as needed 2. nonchlorine bleach as needed
3. do not bleach

DRY-CLEANING

1. ◯ 2.

1. dry-clean 2. do not dry-clean

JOB AND
MONEY
STUFF

How to Write a Résumé

A résumé is the document with all the information—previous jobs, education, skills—that a prospective employer will need to determine that you are, of course, the best candidate for the job. It's like a cheat sheet for your awesomeness. Here's how to write a standout.

- Put contact information at the top. (You want your new boss to be able to reach you with the good news!) Share as many details and links as you're comfortable with, including your Twitter, Skype, or personal website, if relevant/applicable.

- Keep your employment history brief: include only information relevant to the job you're applying for (spare your prospective employer from reading about your high-school snack-bar job), and limit job descriptions to one or two sentences.

- A section about your skills can include any-thing from the languages you speak to the equipment you know how to operate—it de-pends on the job. If you're struggling to think of pertinent items—or how to phrase them—search for job postings in your field and see what they say an ideal candidate should be able to do. If you can do those things, list them.

- Extra information like your GPA, hobbies, athletic awards, or volunteer experience isn't mandatory but can set you apart from the crowd (you never know, you could bond with your interviewer over a mutual love of Latin). Add what you think is best.

Sample Résumé

Name
Address
Phone number, e-mail address

PROFILE
Two to three sentences describing who you are, where you went to school, and what you are currently doing.

EDUCATION
Dates you attended Institution, degree received (most recent first)
Dates you attended Institution, classes taken, honors received

EXPERIENCE
Most recent employer, company description or URL
Start date–end date
Position you held
Responsibilities and other pertinent info

Previous employer, company description or URL
Start date–end date

Position you held

Awards, successful projects, skills you learned while on the job

ADDITIONAL SKILLS
Bulleted list of the following:

- Types of tasks you can accomplish (proof-reading, waitressing, word processing, field research).

- Tools you can use (photo editing software, coding languages, specialized drivers' licenses, lab equipment).

- Qualities you have (time-management skills, interpersonal communication, the ability to learn fast).

INTERESTS AND HOBBIES
A few sentences detailing what you do in your spare time. Some might be relevant to your chosen field, but this section is primarily for humanizing you, giving a bit of flavor to your résumé. Keep it professional and brief.

References available on request

How to Write a Cover Letter

Where a résumé outlines your background and experience, the cover letter is an opportunity to tailor that information to the position you're applying for—adding context—and it's often the first thing a prospective employer will read. No pressure, right? Here's how to rock it.

- Write clearly, concisely, and professionally. Even relaxed informal companies will want a cover letter that is serious and demonstrates your communication skills. Sound like yourself, but your sharpest, smartest self.

- Why do you want the job? (No, "I'm broke" doesn't count.) Why are you the best person for the position? Explain how your previous work applies to this job or why your skills are a perfect fit.

- Even if you're seeking employment in a creative field, keep the cover letter simple and legible. Use a black, basic font in 12-point type, and do not exceed one page (or three medium-sized paragraphs if it's an e-mail letter).

- Read application requirements thoroughly, and answer questions to the best of your ability. Some people may want the cover letter sent as the body of an e-mail, rather than an attachment, or formatted in a particular way. Some postings will ask that you direct your application to a specific human resources contact. Proofread everything—don't lose points for something as trivial as misspelling a name.

- Also mention: where you heard about the job, how you first learned about the organization, mutual connections. (If you know a current or former employee, name them! Just make sure to get their approval first.)

- Dream company isn't hiring? You can still send a cover letter to introduce yourself as a possible employee. All the same rules apply: discuss why you're a good fit for the work and the company, and show off your experience and achievements.

Sample Cover Letter

Name
Address
Phone number
E-mail address

Date

Dear Mr./Ms. [Name],

I am writing to apply for the [job] position that [company] is looking to fill. I heard about the job through [source] and am very interested in the opportunity. I recently graduated from [school] with [degree] and have previously worked as [position] for [organization].

I have extensive experience with [task], and [give details about when and where that took place]. My experience working with [tool] has allowed me to become a valuable member of the team, something I hope to bring to your company as well.

[The next two to three paragraphs should similarly address the job requirements and how you fit them. Back up your achievements with numbers—percentages, results, sales—if you can.]

I have long admired [company] and this position seems like a perfect fit for me. [Elaborate on what you like about the company—show that you really understand what they do, do well, and care about.] I am [a couple of positive adjectives—smart, hardworking, a fast learner, a team player, attentive to detail] and hope you will take my application into consideration. Thank you for your time.

Sincerely,

[Name]

How to Nail an Interview

Congratulations! All that time spent polishing your cover letter and choosing just the right font for your résumé paid off. Now you just need to meet face to face with whoever will be deciding your future—totally *not* terrifying. Prepare with these tips, and all will go smoothly.

Before

- Get the basic information. Know when and where the interview will be taking place, plus any door codes or sign-in instructions you'll need. Ask if the interviewer would like you to bring anything in particular and whether a test will be administered.

- Be on time. Scratch that—be early. Plan your travel route and arrange backup transportation. Be sure you know where in the building you're headed so you don't end up wandering around.

- Skype interview? Test your Internet connection, camera, and microphone ahead of time. (Also, it doesn't hurt to make sure your computer camera is pointed toward your most impressive books.)

- Learn the organization's history and goals. Google-stalk the founder. Read interviews and press releases. Show that you are informed and care about the people you're hoping to work for.

- Prepare answers for the following questions:

    ○ Why you are interested in the job

    ○ Why you are interested in the organization

    ○ What your strengths and weaknesses are

    ○ What you hope to learn

    ○ What your previous experiences bring to this job

○ Why you are the best candidate

○ When you can start/what your schedule is like

○ What the organization does well/what they could be doing better

- Have questions of your own (and no, "when can I start?" doesn't count). It shows that you've put thought into the position and are interested in learning more. Some potential questions:

   ○ Whom will I be reporting to/whom will I be working closely with?

   ○ What are the day-to-day responsibilities? What's a typical workday like?

   ○ What qualities are you looking for in a candidate?

   ○ Is there opportunity for growth within the organization?

   ○ If I wish to learn new skills, is the organization interested in fostering that?

○ Is there anything I can do to make myself a more attractive candidate?

- Wear appropriate, neat, clean, professional clothing (see page 12 for tips). Don't arrive listening to music, drinking coffee, or chewing gum (although a breath mint beforehand is probably a good idea).

During

- Bring all relevant materials. Better yet, bring *all* materials, relevant or otherwise: copies of your résumé and cover letter, work samples, personal business cards and a portfolio if you have them.

- Give a good handshake. Make eye contact and smile, then extend you arm and grasp the interviewer's hand firmly. You don't want to squeeze the person's hand painfully, but a weak, floppy grip is no good either. Shake from the elbow, once, maybe twice.

- Sit upright during the entire interview. You don't want to look like you're about to run away, but now is not the time to kick back and slump in the chair.

- Take time if you need to think up a good response. Repeat after me: "That's a great question, I hadn't considered it before." If you still can't think of something, it's okay to say "I don't know, but I'd hope to learn."

- *Slooooow down.* Remember to breathe. Try to avoid saying "like" and "um" or ending your sentences like a question? And relax, because you're doing great.

After

- Let your interviewer know that you appreciate their time—a handwritten note is never too much! Reiterate how excited you are about the job ("I really enjoyed learning more about your company and the opportunity you're offering"), answer any questions you might not have been able to respond to during the interview ("You had asked me about my web design skills, and I thought you might like to know that..."), and offer to send supplementary material ("I'm happy to provide additional references or work samples").

- Don't write about the interview or job online! Even if you have nothing but good things to say, keep it to yourself. You can always jubilantly take to social media *after* you've secured the position.

- If you don't hear back within a week, send a polite follow-up e-mail. It doesn't have to be elaborate, just a quick word letting them know you're still interested and thinking about the job. You want to keep reminding whoever is making the decision that you exist.

- If you don't get the job, be gracious and don't burn bridges. Thank them for considering you, express that you'd love if they kept you in mind for future openings, and wish them the best with their new employee.

How to Start Your New Job on the Right Foot

Congrats, you got the job! Now what? First impressions can be crucial, so here's how to start a new career stress- and complication-free.

- **Start preparing early.** A new job is stressful so plan ahead to smooth the transition.

    - *The week before:* Decide on outfits for the first few days, shopping for work-appropriate clothes if necessary. Pick up handy office tools, like a spare USB stick or ergonomic mouse pad (tendinitis is real, folks). Adopt a sleep schedule that won't leave you groggy when the alarm bell rings.

    - *The night before:* Pack your bag so that everything is ready to go; don't forget any required paperwork you've been given to fill out. Make a lunch. Go to bed early, and set as many alarms as you need for peace of mind.

○ *The morning of:* Aim to wake up 15–30 minutes earlier than you have to. You never know when disaster will strike, and you absolutely do not want to be late on your first day. Spend a little extra time grooming, and don't forget weather-appropriate extra layers.

- **Introduce yourself.** Even if your superiors introduce you to the entire staff (but especially if they don't!), let everyone know your name and job title. Shake hands, smile, and ask for coworkers' names. You want to assimilate into the work culture as soon as possible, and having people recognize you is the first step.

- **Make friends.** You don't have to be BFFs with Samantha from accounting by the end of your first day, but make an effort to be friendly and personable right off the bat. Work is immeasurably more enjoyable and navigable with friends—you'll learn who always jams the printer and who'll take credit for your work, plus you'll have someone to grab happy hour sangria with.

- **Learn as much as you can.** Ask for a tour of the workspace if it's not offered, including areas like meeting rooms, break areas, and anywhere specialized equipment is kept. Don't hesitate to ask questions. No one expects you to know everything right off the bat. Better to get clarification now than to look incompetent later.

- **Make yourself the ideal employee—but set boundaries.** Take on responsibilities, prove to your bosses that you can be trusted, and give 100 percent effort to doing things properly and efficiently. But if you feel that you're being taken advantage of (say, if the job was described as a typical 9-to-5 and you're routinely being asked to stay until 7 p.m.), you are within your rights to refuse. If you're asked to complete a project in an unrealistic timeline, be polite and accommodating but voice your concerns.

Working from Home 101

More and more people are working from home, and though the flexibility is wonderful, it can be tough to self-manage. To do so successfully, remember the following:

- **Set a schedule.** Dedicate specific hours every day to work.

- **Create a workspace.** It's easier to be productive in a designated work area than sprawled on your bed or slouched on the sofa.

- **Keep talking to your coworkers.** If you don't use a work chat platform, bounce ideas off one another through other means, like Google chat or e-mail.

- **Go dark.** You'll accomplish more without constant interruptions. When you have to, turn off your phone and Wi-Fi connection. (There are even disruption-free word processing programs that will create a more tranquil environment.)

How to Understand Your Paycheck

In a perfect world, your boss would give you a handful of gold doubloons and tell you not to spend it all in one place. But reality is a little more complicated, so here's how to make sense of that piece of paper you get every two weeks.

The basics

A paycheck has two parts: (1) the pay stub notes the pay period (typically the past two weeks), annual salary, deductions, and take-home pay; and (2) the check or a voided check confirms a direct deposit to your bank account.

Gross ≠ disgusting

The total amount of money you've earned before deductions is called the *gross amount*. The take-home amount is called the *net amount*, which brings us to…

Deductions

Lots of things take chunks out of your paycheck: federal tax, any applicable state or local tax, Social Security, and Medicare, for example. If your company provides benefits like a retirement plan, also known as a 401(k), or a pretax fund to pay for transit, your contribution will likely come out of your gross income as well. Your accounts manager should be able to explain unfamiliar acronyms.

Grand totals

Once you've figured out what the different amounts represent, add the numbers to make sure all calculations were made correctly. If you worked overtime or holiday hours, that should be clearly marked in a different row from your regular salary. Paid vacation or sick days will also be split up from your normal hours.

How to Deal with Taxes

No one likes paying taxes. No one. Welcome to adulthood! But they do have to be paid, and if you're organized and informed, the task won't seem so daunting (and you might even save some money).

Wasn't my income already taxed?

Yes, but the amount withheld from your paycheck is essentially a prepayment on the tax you owe the government. Once you've filed your taxes, it'll become clear if you've either over- or underpaid; if it's the former, you'll be getting a refund. Yay!

When do I file?

The federal filing deadline in the United States is April 15 (e.g., the deadline for tax year 2016 is April 15, 2017), but you can file as soon as you have the appropriate paperwork from your employer(s). File as early as you can—your nerves will thank you! If you work freelance or are self-employed, you may need to file taxes once a quarter. Check with your city and state revenue service.

Do I have to file?

In short: yes. If you made any money, you absolutely need to *file* your taxes, even if you might not be able to *pay* them. Otherwise, the government will fine you for both failing to file and failing to pay and will charge interest for every month you're late. You will end up paying, it's just a question of how much.

But I'm unemployed/I still live with my parents!

Even if you're currently camped out in your parents' house watching *The Last Unicorn* for the nineteenth time, you still have to file your taxes. You might think it's useless (or hugely unfair) to be on the hook for tax filing when you're unemployed, but you still have to (particularly if you've been collecting unemployment benefits, which are considered income). You can, however, deduct the costs of looking for work, including travel costs and similar job-seeking expenses.

What paperwork do I need?

If you have a salaried job (i.e., a job where your employer withholds taxes from each paycheck), you should receive a W-2 form from your employer detailing important info like your salary, taxes withheld, and employer ID number. If you do independent contractor work, you should have a form 1099-MISC from every company that has paid you more than $600 in the year. You'll use these forms to fill out a federal form 1040, 1040-EZ (if you have no dependents), or 1040-ES (if you're paying estimated taxes on nonwithheld payments; see above). You can download the forms from irs.gov or file electronically.

If you're working freelance, congratulations, you're self-employed! Unless you've incorporated yourself, your business is considered a sole proprietorship and, along with your regular 1040 form, you'll need to file a Schedule C (or Schedule C-EZ if your expenses total less than $5,000 and you have no inventory and no employees). If your net profit for the year exceeded $400, you'll also need to file for self-employment tax (which means you're filing as employee *and* employer) using Schedule SE.

Additionally, if you plan to claim any deductions (see below), you'll need to keep receipts all year as proof of what you spent your money on. (Making a spreadsheet of monthly expenses can be helpful, but at the least keep hard copies in an envelope somewhere).

Am I a dependent or not?

In the United States, you are considered someone's dependent if you lived in their home for the entire year, received more than 50 percent of your support from them, are a US citizen, national, or resident alien, and earned less than a certain amount that year (usually in the $4,000 range). If these things apply, the person in question may claim you as a dependent and qualify for an exemption. You may still be asked to file your own taxes, though, and you don't get an exemption for *being* someone's dependent.

Do I get any exemptions, deductions, or credits?

Maybe. *Exemptions* are amounts you can automatically subtract from your income based on things like where you live and your marital status. *Deductions* are expenses such as student loans and charitable donations that the government won't tax. *Credits* are amounts taken out of the tax you owe; if you attended school in the past year, have a dependent child, or have a retirement plan, for example, you can take advantage of associated credits. As for deductions, check the "standard deduction" for your tax year: if your total deductions are less than that amount, you can claim the standard deduction and don't have to itemize (i.e., make a list of) all your deductions.

Do I have to write an actual paper check?

It's the 21st century, and you can file your taxes using software designed for that purpose! Government websites will often list approved programs—some with free versions. Sign up for a direct deposit option, if it's available, so that your refund goes directly into your bank account. No matter how you file, make and keep hard copies of all forms.

There's still something I don't get...

If you can afford to, hire an accountant. Otherwise, take to the Internet. Also look up tax advice that is specific to your industry—there might be tips you hadn't considered. And if you earned less than $53,000 in the past year, you qualify for the Volunteer Income Tax Assistance program. They'll help you with your taxes for free.

How to Deal with Insurance

Insurance in a nutshell: you pay a regular fee, or *premium*, to an organization that agrees to pay for damages in case of an accident or theft. If that happens, you'll file a *claim*, usually a list of damages or stolen items, sometimes accompanied by photos. Here's a breakdown of the types of insurance you might need.

Health insurance

Health insurance comes from one of three places: your job, the government, or a plan your purchase as an individual. Your employment and financial situations will dictate which is the best choice for you. Several types of plans exist:

- **Exclusive provider organization (EPO):** a plan in which services are covered only if you use doctors and facilities in the plan's network. (Emergency situations are the exception.)

- **Health maintenance organization (HMO):** Similarly to EPOs, an HMO will likely cover care only from doctors who work with it. You may be required to live or work in the HMO's service area, and the focus is often on preventative care.

- **Point of service (POS):** A POS will provide you with a list of primary physicians whom you have to visit in order to be referred to other doctors (often specialists). You have the option of seeing doctors outside the POS network, but you'll pay more out of pocket.

- **Preferred provider organization (PPO):** A PPO gives you the choice of visiting doctors both in and out of the network. You will pay more if you choose to go outside the network, but you don't need a referral from your primary care doctor.

No matter how invincible you feel, having health insurance is a good idea. If you're under the age of twenty-six, you may qualify for coverage under your parents' insurance. If you're a US citizen, you can sign up for a plan through the federal health insurance marketplace at healthcare.gov, but only during the time of year designated as an "open enrollment period."

Car insurance

If you own a car, you must have *liability insurance*—it's legally required almost everywhere in the US and Canada. This type of auto insurance covers anything you as a driver are liable for after an accident, like medical bills and property damage.

If you want insurance to cover repairs to your car after an accident, you'll want *collision coverage*—not legally required and perhaps not worth it if your car is older.

Comprehensive coverage will cover damage done to your car from things other than collisions, like weather mishaps, one-car accidents (like if you hit a deer), and theft.

Personal injury protection will pay for medical bills for you and your passengers, regardless of who was at fault in an accident.

Young people tend to pay a higher auto premium (sorry!), but you can minimize costs by driving safely (more accidents = riskier to insure = more \$\$) and driving a "safe" car (i.e., a gently used sedan instead of a flashy new convertible).

Renter's insurance

Renter's, or tenant's, insurance covers loss of possessions to fire, flood, or theft. It can also cover things like hotel stays if your landlord decides to fumigate the building.

Though often required by the terms of a lease, renter's insurance is a good idea regardless: an average payment of \$12 a month will get you around \$30,000 worth of coverage.

Pay close attention to what your policy includes: things like earthquakes aren't always covered. Keep an inventory list of everything you own to make filing claims go smoothly.

Possession insurance

Expensive items that could be stolen or damaged are often insured individually, since renter's insurance coverage caps how much you can claim for individual objects.

If you have your great-grandma's diamond necklace lying around, by all means insure it, but also consider expensive items that you need for work—power tools, musical instruments, electronics, etc.

Other Types of Insurance

Shelling out for things like life insurance, travel insurance, and pet insurance might seem smart, but resist the urge to overbuy. Unless you have dependents, for example, you probably don't need life insurance. Not sure? Make a pros and cons list to see if it's worth budgeting for.

How to Make (and Stick to) a Basic Budget

Spending without thinking is incredibly easy (and sometimes fun), but being organized and responsible with your money will spare you overdraft fees and maybe even allow you to save up for big purchases (or, um, retirement).

1. Calculate your income.

Got a steady paycheck? This part's easy. Working part-time, flexible hours, or free-lance? Calculate a busy month, then do the same for a dry spell, and split the difference to find your average monthly income.

2. Calculate your fixed expenses.

Fixed means stuff you pay for every month, without exception: rent, food, utilities, insur-ance, and transportation costs. Include things like student loans, car payments, and 401(k) contributions if applicable.

3. Subtract expenses from income.
Ideally, you should have some money left over (if not, go back and check your math!). This is your *expendable income*, which you can divvy up for other (read: fun) expenses.

4. Keep track of how you spend.
Set up a monthly spreadsheet in a program like Microsoft Excel to track how you're spending that expendable income. Group or even color-code your expenses in broad categories: food, entertainment, home (rent, utilities, repairs), pets, fitness, work, and travel.

5. Tweak as necessary.
Running into the red? Assign limits to your disposable-income categories and stick to them. Small changes, like making coffee at home instead of spending $6 on Starbucks, visiting your library instead of buying books, or packing a lunch, make a big difference.

6. Save early, save often.
The goal of a budget is not to end up with a balanced zero dollars in your bank account at month's end. Once your spending habits

are under control, start a savings account and earmark a little cash every month for emergencies—a parking ticket, surgery for your pet, a replacement computer—or long-term goals like a down payment on a car or house. Even if you won't be saving hundreds of dollars every month, having a nest egg will provide peace of mind.

7. **Handle windfalls wisely.**
Earn a big bonus at work, receive an unexpected inheritance, or win the lottery? (It could happen!) Put the money toward outstanding debt *before* spending it on fun stuff.

How to Use a Credit Card Responsibly

A credit card is a good idea: it's convenient, it helps you establish good credit (if you pay it off), and it can save you in an emergency. But spending responsibility will ensure your dream of owning a home isn't stymied because of a few shopping-spree-related indiscretions.

- Get *a* credit card, not *twelve*. (If frequent spending puts you over the credit limit of one card, it's time to reprioritize.) Shop around so you don't end up slapped with ridiculous annual fees. You can also apply for a credit line at your bank.

- Read the fine print. Your credit limit is how much you're allowed to spend—don't exceed it! Your annual percentage rate (APR) is the amount charged if you carry over the previous month's balance (that is, you don't pay off all that you owe). Watch for fees; sometimes they don't kick in for six months to a year.

- A credit card is not a blank check. Use it to buy things you *need*, not stuff you want. The minute you use your card, you should already be thinking about paying it off.

- Don't make only the minimum payment. Pay your balance. Every. Month. Interest and late fees stack up fast, and you run the risk of ending up with bad credit.

- Don't use a credit card to get cash at an ATM unless it's an emergency. Interest rates on cash withdrawals tend to be—and this is the industry term—bananas.

- Rewards programs can be an easy way to accumulate extra cash or help pay for your next flight. But again, always read the fine print: look out for catches like annual fees and spending minimums.

- Can't make your monthly payment? Let your creditor know ahead of time and you may work out an alternate payment plan. If you've been receiving more attractive card offers, try to renegotiate your interest rate so they can keep your business.

- Keep old cards active and paid off, even if you never use them. Part of your credit score is determined by the length of your credit history, and closing old accounts can have a detrimental effect.

How to Buy a Car

A car is one of the biggest purchases—physically and financially—you'll ever make. Knowing what you want and being informed will save you from getting ripped off or ending up with a subpar vehicle. Here's how to shop like a pro.

- Make a list (yes, on paper!) of what you want in terms of size, fuel efficiency, cost, ecofriendliness, transmission type, and mileage (if the car is used).

- A car is not a one-and-done purchase. When budgeting, consider monthly insurance premiums, title transfer and inspection fees, and fuel and repair costs.

- Consider buying used. New cars lose value just rolling out of the lot, and used cars—even those in pretty good shape—come much cheaper. Get the car's full vehicular pedigree—including the number of owners, accident history, any previous mechanical problems, and what repairs and maintenance have been done—from a third-party service like CarFax.

- Financing lets you pay a little at a time, as opposed to paying the full amount in cash, but usually involves spending more than the sticker price because of interest rates. Do the math first!

- Don't buy the first car you see, or even the fifth. Visit dealerships, browse online, and get an idea of prices and quality. Start shopping with no intention of buying: you can (and should) walk away for a day or two before signing on the dotted line. If anyone makes you feel pressured or guilty, or if the negotiation isn't going well, go elsewhere.

- And speaking of negotiating: once you've made a decision, don't accept the initial price. Use a resource like NADAguides.com or the Kelley Blue Book to figure out the approximate price the dealer paid for the car—your first offer shouldn't be too much higher than that. Negotiate the "out-the-door price": the price with everything, even taxes, included.

Nervous to haggle in person? Negotiate over e-mail, and tell dealers that you'll come in person to sign paperwork only once the price is set.

- Car salespeople aren't as slimy as the stereotype, but you should keep your wits about you. Don't take anything a dealer says at face value, and don't let them play on your emotions (you can even ask them to be quiet during a test drive if they're pointing out too many perks).

- Read absolutely everything you sign. Don't agree to extra fees that may be tacked on at the end, and don't sign an "as is" statement (a document that states you agree to buy the car in whatever shape it's in at the moment). Make sure you get thirty days to test the car and return it if there are hidden flaws.

SOCIAL
STUFF

How to Make New Friends

Lonely? Bored? You are not alone—literally. Almost everyone feels this way postgraduation, and while forging friendships was easier in college, plenty of youngish people *are* out there and eager to make new friends. Here's how to find 'em.

- **Get a hobby.** Joining interest-specific groups gives you an in with like-minded people. Check for flyers at your gym, library, or coffee shop, or hit up websites like Meetup.com to find everything from board game nights to knitting clubs.

- **Volunteer.** Help causes you care about while meeting other cool people. Meals-on-wheels programs and no-kill animal shelters always need help—and there's no better ice-breaker than playing with adorable kittens.

- **Scour the Internet.** Some dating sites let you search for platonic companionship—just make that clear to anyone who messages you! You might be surprised by who else is looking for cuddle-free bonding.

- **Poach from existing friends.** Ask a better-established bud to introduce you to their social circle to meet preapproved potential pals.

- **Join your school's alumni network.** Many colleges organize cocktail parties or outings for alumni, particularly in cities with large numbers of former students. Check the school's website, or contact your alma mater directly—at least you'll get some wine and cheese out of it!

- **Support an institution.** Museums, libraries, and arts organizations are always after a younger crowd, so look into whether your city's cultural hotspots host special programs for the 18- to 35-year-old demo.

- **Coworkers are fair game.** Grab drinks after work with colleagues—you'll bond and commiserate, and your workdays will become more enjoyable. Or invite officemates to lunch once in a while (inventing something like "Taco Tuesdays" is goofy, but it works!).

- **Be proactive...** You'll have to make more of an effort to cultivate friendships than ever before, and that's all right. You don't need to be seducing these proto-pals, but do reach out to people, suggest activities, make definite plans, and follow up. Say "yes" and go out when invited. It all starts somewhere.

- **...but don't be too hard on yourself.** You won't hit it off with everyone you meet—right away, or ever. But if making new friends takes time, it's never been easier to keep in touch with your old ones.

How to Host a Dinner Party

Congratulations, you're about to entertain! Nothing says "I'm a functional adult" quite like inviting friends over for a mature evening of food and conversation. These tips will make the whole endeavor a rousing success.

- **Figure out the scope.** Decide how many guests are attending and how much work you're willing to put into the affair. Will this be a sit-down dinner or a the-more-the-merrier-style potluck? Manage everyone's expectations.

- **Send invitations.** Handwritten notes not necessary! Share the deets on Facebook or by e-mail: what kind of meal you're serving, what guests should bring (if anything), and whether plus-ones are welcome.

- **For potlucks, plan ahead.** Coordinate with guests so that you don't end up with fourteen baguettes and no vegetables. Stock up on serving spoons—not everyone will remember to bring one—and ask everyone to label dishes for easy returning.

- **Keep the menu simple.** Avoid new-to-you recipes or anything that must be cooked in batches (no made-to-order omelets!) unless you want to be stuck in the kitchen all night. Be mindful of allergies, religious preferences, and dietary restrictions: a good host ensures everyone eats comfortably.

- **Shop early and smart.** Stock up ahead of time—you don't want to be running to stores the morning of the dinner party—and make sure you have staples like flour, oil, and sugar.

- **Get equipped.** Do you have all the requisite kitchen supplies? Enough dishes, glassware, cutlery, and seating? Borrow or buy whatever you need, and don't forget small essentials like ice and napkins (and, *ahem*, toilet paper).

- **Make a schedule.** Give yourself more time than you think you need to get all the food ready. Pay attention to the cooking times of recipes and do prep work as soon as you can (chop ingredients ahead of time, put in a bowl, and store in the fridge until needed). Bake desserts ahead (the morning of, or earlier) and pick no-cook appetizers for guests to munch on while waiting for the meal.

- **Set the mood.** Create ambiance with a playlist that's a few hours long and lively but not fist-pumpingly upbeat. Light a few candles, use a nice tablecloth, and if you have flowers or decorations you can use as a centerpiece, pull 'em out.

- **Host.** Your job isn't over once the food is out. Introduce guests to one another and help start conversations. If a wallflower is having a hard time mingling, pay attention to them for a while.

- **Take your time.** Don't immediately clean up after the food's gone. Linger at the table, make sure the conversation is flowing (by encouraging some and reining in others), and start washing dishes only once everyone has left.

How to Ask Someone Out

Asking a cute human being to go on a date is one of the hardest things: you're putting yourself out there and risking rejection. But the rewards are worth it. Here's how to pull it off successfully, you Casanova, you.

- **Make your interest clear.** Don't say you want to *hang out*. The object of your affection might think you mean spending time as friends. Make your request clear by asking, "May I take you out for dinner or drinks?" or by using the word *date*.

- **Keep things casual to start.** Work in your invitation near the end of a conversation, or send a quick text or online message. Sure, an in-person request is more special, but if you're having trouble getting the words out, sending a quick "Hey, would you be interested…" message is absolutely valid.

- **If yes, make firm plans.** No one wants to get asked to do "something" "sometime"—suggest a specific time and place. "Dinner and a movie" may be standard, but grabbing drinks or coffee is a better first-date option: it's casual and low commitment, and if things get awkward, you don't have to stick around for dessert or the closing credits. Sign off with a simple, optimistic "Can't wait!"

- **If no, handle rejection gracefully.** Getting turned down sucks, but remember that your crush doesn't owe you anything. *You* might think you're a match made in heaven, but the object of your affection is not required to date you or even to tell you *why* they're not interested. Say something along the lines of "Okay, no worries, have a good night," and don't push. Eventually you'll find someone who jumps at the chance to get to know you better.

Online Dating 101

Giving Internet dating a try? Once you've browsed your matches and found an appealing candidate, chat online for a bit and get to know the person. If DogLuvr25 seems engaging, no red flags fly (*btw im married*), and you'd like to meet in real life, suggest getting together. If you're comfortable, send your cell number to make coordinating easier: "We should get drinks. Friday? I'm at (XXX) XXX-XXX." Pick a place that's public (safety first!) and convenient for both of you, and tell a friend where you're headed. Then have fun! If the date's a dud, it's fine to send a quick text the next day: "That was great, but I don't think we're a fit." If your online cutie says no, don't take it personally. You have plenty more profiles to go through.

How to Break Up with Someone

If you thought asking someone out was hard, great news—ending a relationship can be even harder! If you've gotta go, do it maturely and respectfully, like the grownup you are.

- **Think about why you've come to this decision...** Don't do anything rash. Consider the pros and cons of the relationship and paint a clear picture, which will help you explain to your partner why you're no longer satisfied.

- **...and then do it.** Once you've decided, don't avoid the conversation, daunting as it is. Stringing someone along is unfair. Be kind and mindful of your timing—no one wants to get dumped after, say, being fired or going to their grandmother's funeral.

- **Talk in person, if possible.** Sit your partner down, preferably in a private place (they might cry), and explain your reasons. As when asking someone out (page 132), be clear: say that you want to break up. If you can't meet face to face, call or Skype.

- **Honest doesn't mean harsh.** Be constructive, diplomatic, and gentle, and for the love of whatever you find holy, stay away from *it's-not-you-it's-me* clichés. Try "I need [thing that you need], and this relationship no longer fulfills it." Apologize for causing pain, and listen to what they have to say (unless they lash out and say nasty things. Be ready for that, too).

- **Give it time.** Cutting off all communication isn't always practicable: your ex might need to pick up stuff from your place or want to apologize. But postbreakup time apart *is* crucial, so even if the split is totally amicable, give each other space. If you want to be friends (though it's okay if you don't), it won't happen overnight—and jumping into friendship too quickly can lead your ex on.

- **Done seeing someone casually?** You've gone on a few dates and things went pretty well, but you aren't feeling it and don't want to invest further time and effort. That's fine, but *tell this person* you're done. No one likes to be on the receiving end of the fade out (you know, when the person you were excited about suddenly drops off the face of the earth and doesn't return your texts). No big, sit-down conversation required: you can deal with it on a final date or in a text message when they ask you out again. Be nice but firm: "I've been having fun with you, but I honestly don't see this turning into a relationship, so I don't think we should go out again."

- **End an abusive relationship.** Whether the hurt is physical, emotional, sexual, or psychological, abusive relationships can be extremely damaging, even dangerous. If you are in—or think you're in—this type of situation but don't know how to leave, call the National Domestic Violence Hotline (1-800-799-SAFE). They can help you end the relationship safely.

How to Attend a Wedding

It's a fact of life: as people get older, people get married. And that's a good thing! Weddings are parties, a fun celebration of a wonderful milestone in the life of people you care about. And as with any institution that's been around a while, rules must be followed. Here's how conduct yourself so that everyone has a good time.

- **Confirm your attendance.** This is about more than being polite: a large wedding is a carefully orchestrated affair, and knowing the exact number of attendees is necessary. If the invitation notes an "RSVP by" date, respect it and let the couple know if you'll attend and whether you'll bring a date—if you've been offered that option (your invitation will be addressed to "Mr./Ms. [your name] and Guest" if so). Don't assume that a plus-one (or child) is welcome. If you have to cancel at the last minute, definitely alert the couple.

- **Give a gift.** If you attend the wedding, you should give a gift, period. The easiest way is to shop the couple's gift registry (usually listed on the invitation) for something within your budget, though a check with a nice card is fine. If you won't be attending, technically you're off the hook, but sending a card wishing them well is a nice gesture. Procrastinator? Conventional wedding etiquette allows you to give a gift up to a year after the wedding.

- **Be a team player.** If you're asked to be a part of the wedding as a bridesmaid, groomsman, or anything in between, congratulations! Before you commit, ask what the happy couple requires of you. You might be expected to attend dress shopping trips and prewedding festivities like bridal showers, bachelor parties, etc. Better to bow out early than be blindsided by a bride who expects you to buy a custom-made dress or a couple who presume you have an entire week to devote to their nuptials.

- **Dress the part.** The invitation should specify a dress code, but if not, a suit or cocktail dress will do the trick. Avoid wearing white (that's for the bride!), and use judgment with black—traditionally, it's reserved for funerals. If the ceremony will be at a religious site, dress appropriately—collars and ties, no bare shoulders or short hems. And wear shoes you can dance in!

- **Set boundaries...** Don't feel pressure to spend money you don't have on a destination wedding and endless bridal party events. If you're uncomfortable with portions of the proceedings (anything from a seedy bachelor party to a religious prayer), feel free to excuse yourself.

- **...but remember that it's not about you.** The bride might be bossy, the theme might be ridiculous, and the bar might be cash, but guess what: it's *their* special day. Be gracious. Don't snicker during speeches, stick around until the cake is cut, and thank the couple for inviting you, either during the receiving line (if there is one) or before the end of the night.

Social Media Etiquette 101

Every site or service will be a little different (the way you use Snapchat will likely differ from your LinkedIn behavior, and your Reddit presence might bear little resemblance to your Pinterest boards), but these ten easy steps will help you conduct yourself like a decent, informed human on the Internet.

1. Never post anything you wouldn't say to someone's face.

2. Use spellcheck, pay attention to homophones like "their" and "they're" and "there," and punctuate correctly.

3. Cut down on cussing, especially if you're arguing with someone. Do you have to give up swearing? Hell, no! Just be judicious.

4. Jokes (well, "jokes") about gender, race, ethnicity, weight, or sexuality are a bad idea.

Even if you're trying to be ironic, your witticisms may not be received that way.

5. If friends are talking about something you don't understand (events, terminology, philosophy, etc.), don't waste their time asking for an explanation; look it up. You have a wealth of information at your fingertips—this is the Internet, after all.

6. Don't overshare. If you need to disclose intimate ins and outs, start a group message with close friends.

7. Don't use the Internet to hash out real-life problems. (You're classier than that!) And avoid passive-aggressive updates like "Some people don't understand the meaning of loyalty." That's not dealing with disagreement constructively; it's just rude and mean.

8. If you need to cut ties with someone, go ahead and unfriend and/or block the person. Give your privacy settings the once-over to make sure you're properly protected, and don't hesitate to report someone if you feel

harassed. If someone you can't unfriend is bothering you, subtly unfollow the person to avoid seeing their unpleasant diatribes.

9. Be safe. Don't post pictures of your current surroundings, particularly if you're in a public place, and never share information like your address or phone number in a public feed. Protecting your account or limiting your privacy settings helps but is not foolproof.

10. Be yourself. You're cool and fun and interesting offline, so let your Internet persona be that same lovable weirdo.

Acknowledgments

I would like to thank my parents, who taught me valuable life lessons; my brothers, who seem to think I've absorbed those lessons; and my friends, who fill in the gaps when needed.

Thank you to everyone at Quirk Books (you have all been a joy to work with) and everyone who thought, throughout my academic and professional career, that my ideas were good and my words worth reading.